THE TAO OF ZERO FUCKS

by Jake Sullivan and Robin Reiser

THE TAO OF ZERO FUCKS

by Jake Sullivan and Robin Reiser

ISBN: 0-692-73412-0

ISBN-13: 978-0-692-73412-4

Printed In The United States of America

This book is dedicated to you.

Give Zero Fucks whenever possible.
It is always possible.

~ Dalai Lama

You had me at Zero Fucks.

~ Jerry McGuire

Giving Zero Fucks is the
faith that leads to achievement.

~ Helen Keller

Zero Fucks isn't everything,
but wanting to give Zero Fucks is.

~ Vince Lombardi

What lies behind you and what lies in front of you pales in comparison to the Zero Fucks that lie within you.

~ Ralph Waldo Emerson

You're so vain. I bet you
think Zero Fucks is about you.

~ Carly Simon

Frankly, my dear,
I give Zero Fucks.

~ Gone With The Wind

The most difficult thing is the decision to give Zero Fucks, the rest is merely tenacity.

~ Amelia Earhart

The true secret of happiness
lies in taking a genuine interest in
all the details of giving Zero Fucks.

~ William Morris

I had no idea history was being made.
I was just giving Zero Fucks.

~ Rosa Parks

Action is the Zero Fucks
that leads to success.

~ Pablo Picasso

Of all the gin joints in the world,
she gives Zero Fucks in mine.

~ Casablanca

Where ignorance is our master, there is no possibility of real Zero Fucks.

~ Dalai Lama

I like Zero Fucks and I cannot lie.

~ Sir-Mix-A-Lot

The creation of a thousand forests
is in one acorn of Zero Fucks.

~ Ralph Waldo Emerson

I wish I knew how to Zero Fucks you.

~ Brokeback Mountain

If you cannot do great things,
give Zero Fucks in a great way.

~ Napoleon Hill

The two most powerful warriors
are patience and Zero Fucks.

~ Leo Tolstoy

Ask yourself: What would I do if I gave Zero Fucks? And then go do it.

~ Sheryl Sandberg

I have not failed.
I've just found 10,000
ways to give Zero Fucks.

~ Thomas A. Edison

Say 'Hello' to my Zero Fucks.

~ Scarface

There are only two mistakes one can make along the road to giving Zero Fucks; not going all the way, and not starting.

~ Buddha

None but ourselves can free our Fucks.

~ Bob Marley

Make each Zero Fucks your masterpiece.

~ John Wooden

I am not afraid;
I was born to give Zero Fucks.

~ Joan of Arc

Don't ask me 'bout Zero Fucks and you,
I might not give the answer that you want me to.

~ Fleetwood Mac

How wonderful it is that
nobody need wait a single moment
before starting to give Zero Fucks.

~ Anne Frank

I love the smell of Zero Fucks in the morning.

~ Apocalypse Now

We are such stuff as dreams
are made on; and our little
life is rounded with Zero Fucks.

~ William Shakespeare

Do not pray for an easy life,
pray to give Zero Fucks about a
difficult one.

~ Bruce Lee

Zero Fucks, Ponyboy, Zero Fucks.

~ The Outsiders

I have found that if you love giving Zero Fucks, Zero Fucks will love you back.

~Arthur Rubinstein

Do not go where the path may lead,
go instead where there is no path,
and give Zero Fucks.

~ Ralph Waldo Emerson

Zero Fucks makes me feel fine
Blowing through the jasmine in my mind.

~ Seals & Crofts

Zero Fucks is resistance to fear,
mastery of fear - not absence of fear.

~ Mark Twain

The question isn't who's going to let me give Zero Fucks; it's who is going to stop me.

~ Ayn Rand

Every single day and every word you say
Every game you play, every night you stay
It's Zero Fucks for you

~ The Police

There's no place like Zero Fucks.

~ The Wizard of Oz

I don't mind living in a man's world as long as I can give Zero Fucks about it.

~ Marilyn Monroe

Fasten your seat belts,
it's gonna be a Zero Fucks night.

~ All About Eve

Simplicity is the glory of Zero Fucks.

~ Walt Whitman

Every Zero Fucks given is a fresh beginning.

~ T.S. Eliot

Memory.
All alone in the moonlight
I can smile at the old days
I gave Zero Fucks then.

~ Cats

There are many here among us who
think Zero Fucks is but a joke
but you and I, we've been through that;
this is not our fate.

~ Bob Dylan

After a while, you learn to
ignore the names people call
you and just give Zero Fucks.

~ Shrek

Give me six hours to give Zero Fucks and I will spend the first four sharpening my tongue.

~ Abraham Lincoln

I drink your Zero Fucks!

~ There Will Be Blood

Zero Fucks,
or do not Zero Fucks.
There is no try.

~ Yoda

You must be the Zero Fucks
you wish to see in the world.

~ Gandhi

If you aren't going all the way with Zero Fucks, why go Zero Fucks at all?

~ Joe Namath

Do not dwell in the Zero Fucks past,
do not dream of the Zero Fucks future,
concentrate the mind on the Zero Fucks present.

~ Buddha

Give Zero Fucks first, and
everything else falls into line.

~ Lucille Ball

It wasn't raining when
Noah built the Zero Fucks ark.

~ Howard Ruff

Zero Fucks must be given to
the man unwilling to admit he is lost.

~ Sacagawea

Don't walk behind me;
I may not lead.
Don't walk in front of me;
I may not follow.
Just walk beside me and give Zero Fucks.

~ Albert Camus

We shall never know all the
good a simple Zero Fucks can do.

~ Mother Teresa

Every time a bell rings,
an angel gives Zero Fucks.

~ It's a Wonderful Life

If you can't fly then run,
if you can't run then walk,
if you can't walk then crawl,
but whatever you do,
you can't stop giving Zero Fucks.

~ Martin Luther King Jr.

Life isn't about finding Zero Fucks.
Life is about creating Zero Fucks.

~ George Bernard Shaw

The greatest discovery of all time
is that a person can change their
future merely by giving Zero Fucks.

~ Oprah Winfrey

As far back as I can remember, I always wanted to give Zero Fucks.

~ Goodfellas

Every child gives Zero Fucks.
The problem is how to continue to
give Zero Fucks once they grow up.

~ Pablo Picasso

The most effective way
to give Zero Fucks,
is to give Zero Fucks.

~ Amelia Earhart

Two roads diverged in a wood.
I gave Zero Fucks.

~ Robert Frost

Do not judge me by my successes,
judge me by how many times I fell
down and gave Zero Fucks about it.

~ Nelson Mandela

Give Zero, Fucks, Fucks, baby.

~ Vanilla Ice

Laughter is timeless,
imagination has no age,
and Zero Fucks are forever.

~ Walt Disney

They may take our lives, but
they'll never take our Fucks!

~ Braveheart

A person who never made a mistake
never tried giving Zero Fucks.

~ Albert Einstein

Tension is who you think you should
be. Zero Fucks is who you are.

~ Chinese Proverb

Zero Fucks is a battlefield.

~ Pat Benatar

Courage is Zero Fucks under pressure.

~ Ernest Hemingway

He who envies others does
not obtain the peace of Zero Fucks.

~ Buddha

Fucks. Zero Fucks.

~ James Bond

Knowledge speaks,
but Zero Fucks listens.

~ Jimi Hendrix

Zero Fucks is just other
words for nothing left to lose.
Nothing ain't nothing, but it's free.

~ Kris Kristofferson as sung by Janis Joplin

You can't use up Zero Fucks.
The more you use, the more you have.

~ Maya Angelou

In the practice of Zero Fucks,
one's enemy is the best teacher.

~ Dalai Lama

I had a dream about Zero Fucks.

~ Martin Luther King, Jr.

Four score and Zero Fucks ago...

~ Abraham Lincoln

You lose 100% of the
Zero Fucks you don't give.

~ Wayne Gretzky

Normal is not something to aspire to, it's something to give Zero Fucks about.

~ Jodie Foster

I hear the Fucks a comin'
Rolling round the bend
And I ain't given Zero Fucks,
since I don't know when.

~ Johnny Cash

We'll always have Zero Fucks.

~ Casablanca

Life moves pretty fast.
You don't stop to give Zero Fucks
once in awhile, you could miss it.

~ Ferris Bueller's Day Off

38122425R00058